ART

19

APOCALYPSE

ARTAUD

1937

APOCALYPSE

Letters from Ireland by

Antonin Artaud

14 August to 21 September 1937

Prefaced by
The New Revelations of Being
Manifesto text: June 1937

Translated and edited
by Stephen Barber
with an Afterword

DIAPHANES

CONTENTS

Les nouvelles révélations de L'ÊTRE

The New Revelations of Being

of Being

Manifesto text: June 1937

Le feu dans l'eau,
                    l'air dans la terre,
l'eau dans l'air
                    et la terre dans la mer.

Ils ne sont pas encore assez fous, ils
ne se sont pas assez rués les uns contre
les autres, et d'autant plus furieux,
d'autant plus enragés qu'ils sont plus
proches et plus familiers.

Là où la Mère mange ses fils,
La Puissance mange la Puissance :
Sans la guerre pas de stabilité.

The fire in the water,
                    the air in the earth,
the water in the air,
                    and the earth in the sea.

They are not yet maddened enough, they are not
yet unleashed enough, one against the other, and
the more furious they are and the more enraged, the
closer and the more intimate they become.

There, where the Mother eats her sons,
Power eats Power:
Without war, no stability.

THE NEW REVELATIONS OF BEING

I say what I have seen and what I believe; and whoever says I have not seen what I have seen, I will now
tear off their head.

Because I am a Brute who cannot be forgiven, and
it will be that way until Time is no longer Time.

Neither Heaven nor Hell, if they exist, can combat
that brutality that they forced onto me, perhaps in
order that I would serve them… Who knows?

In any case, so I would tear myself away from them.

That which is, I see it with certainty. That which is
not, I will make it myself, if I have to.

I have felt the Void for a long time now, but for all
that time, I have refused to throw myself into the
Void.

I have been cowardly, like everything that I see.

I believed for all time that I was refusing this
world, but I know now that I was refusing the Void.

Because I know that this world does not exist and I
know *how* it does not exist.

What I suffered from until now, is that I refused
the Void.

The Void that was already inside of me.

I know that I needed to be illuminated by the Void
and I refused to allow myself to be illuminated.

If I have been made into a living pyre, it was in
order to cure me from being in the world.

And the world took everything away from me.

I struggled to try to exist, to try to subjugate myself

to the forms (to all of the forms) by which the delirious illusion of being in the world screened reality.

I no longer want to be someone subjugated to Illusion.

Dead to the world; to that which constitutes the world for everyone else – fallen at last, fallen, propelled upwards in this void that I had been refusing, now I have a body which undergoes the world, and disgorges reality.

I have had enough of this movement of the moon which makes me call out for what I refuse and refuse what I call out for.

I have to end it. I have to cut myself away from this world that a Being in me, this Being which I can no longer call out for – because if that Being arrives, I will fall into the Void, that this Being always refused.

It's done. I really fell into the Void from the exact moment when everything – everything that makes up this world – just succeeded in rendering me desperate.

Because you never know that you are no longer in this world until you see that you have now truly left it.

The Dead – the others are not separated: they are still revolving around their own dead bodies.

And I know how the dead have been revolving around their own dead bodies for the exact duration of thirty-three Centuries that my own Double never stopped turning.

And, no longer existing, I see what exists.

I truly identified with that Being, that Being that ceased to exist.

And that Being has revealed everything to me.

I knew it all already, but I could not say it, and if I can start to say it now, it is because I have left reality behind.

It is a true Desperate One who is speaking to you and who knows the happiness of being in the world only now that he has left the world behind, now that he has become absolutely separated from it.

The Dead – the others are not separated. They are still turning around their own dead bodies.

I am not dead, but I am separated.

I will therefore say what I have seen and what is...

Artaud at the café Dome in Paris
shortly before his departure for Ireland
Anonymous photographer

Letters

from Ireland

14 August to 21 September 1937

[Note: Throughout this book, Artaud's idiosyncratic use of capital letters is followed.
Words in italics are those which Artaud underlined in his handwritten letters.]

To René Thomas,

14 August 1937

(Postcard, sent from Cobh port, County Cork)

14 August 1937
10 in the morning
Ireland.

Antonin Artaud.

To André Breton,

14 August 1937

(POSTCARD, SENT FROM COBH PORT, COUNTY CORK)

Ireland
14 August 1937.

Antonin Artaud.

To André Breton,

17 August 1937

(Postcard, sent from Galway)

Galway
17 August 1937.

Antonin Artaud.

TO ANNE MANSON,

23 AUGUST 1937

(LETTER, PARTLY LOST, SENT FROM KILRONAN PORT, INISHMORE ISLAND)

[...] Destiny are written in a book,
   and this book is at the Bibliothèque Nationale and has been there for many years.
   Anne, My Life is the realization of a Prophecy.
   One day you will understand my words.
   Know that you will be forever in my heart.
   I embrace you, as we embraced in the Rue Guéné-gaud.

   ANTONIN ARTAUD.

Never lose your fountain pen. It too contains something special. It will protect you and you will be able to touch it.

Mail General Delivery
Kilronan
Inishmore
Aran Islands
Ireland

[Note: Only the last page of the letter has survived.]

To Jean Paulhan,

23 August 1937

(Letter, sent from Kilronan port,
Inishmore island)

Kilronan,
23 August 1937.

I am going to need to find somewhere in the region of 400 francs or so, to go to a place where I have to go, here in Ireland. If there is a way for me to have them by any means whatsoever, you are going to have to send them to me urgently:

> Mail General Delivery
> At Kilronan
> Inishmore
> Aran Islands
> Ireland.

In any case – thank you, because several times in the past you have wanted to help me.

ANTONIN ARTAUD.

Mail General Delivery
Kilronan
Inishmore
Aran Islands
Ireland

Kilronan,
23 August 1937.

Very dear friend,

I've seen that life in Ireland is horrendously expensive!

I doubt that in the cities you could get by on less than one pound a day.

Here where I am, you would pay one pound a week – there are 9 houses, 3 shrubs in the cemetery, and it would take you + 2 hours of walking to reach the village of Kilronan, where there's a post-office, 4 hotels, 2 alcohol stores and around sixty or so houses. The boat from mainland Ireland stops here twice a week.

So those are the practical details.

Now, are you entirely certain that you will not be deeply involved in the World's Momentous Events until three years from now, that's to say from 1940? You will be involved, in the full sight and knowledge of everyone, perhaps. But it seems to me that very shortly from now you will enter into a New Path, which will moreover be your true Path.

Just remember what I said to you one evening:

'there exists in you such a spirit of justice, that it is inconceivable to me that it could remain unused in connection with others, and that it will not manifest itself one day in front of a huge number of people'.

If I've been insistent in telling you on several occasions how I've been struck by the profound feeling of human integrity and of enlightened justice that I can identify in you, it's been no kind of flattery, but instead a prediction that I was making to you in a covert form.

Yours,

ANTONIN ARTAUD

It's probable that many things are going to disturb you and repel you, from the very first sight and moment, in what is now going to be accomplished. But your profound sense of justice will enable you to rise above all that – because this time the end is going to burn up the means.

[Notes: The place Artaud describes at the beginning of the letter is the hamlet of Eoghanacht on the island of Inishmore. Artaud mailed this letter in an envelope he had carried with him from Paris, with the imprint of one of his preferred cafes, the Café Flore.]

(Letter, sent from Galway)

Very dear friend,

I am sure that momentous events are about to happen in the near future, and that you are going to be a determining figure in leading them.

You are, in effect, going to be deeply involved in those Events at the same time as I will be, but not always in the *same* location.

A woman of your acquaintance, who represents High capitalism, will believe herself to be a kind of Théroigne de Mericourt in her involvements with the impending upheavals. She will incite a calamitous Insurrection, in which all of the forces of the left will band together, in a strange alliance also with Jewish High capitalism, and *perhaps even with catholic High capitalism*.

That insurrection will then be pulverised with implacable rigour.

The New Théroigne will have to flee. If she is captured, she will be PUBLICLY MASSACRED. It's possible that she will be able to flee. The woman I'm talking about is X. She's burning with anger at the moment because of what I wrote to her, and she wants people to believe – and to make herself believe – that I'm nothing but a bad actor and a charlatan.

You are going to have your moment of glory, my dear André Breton – you who have always known how to show such a deep affection towards me, such a complete and committed affection.

The World is going to have to bleed as payment for the crime of having been *knowingly* misled about Nature and Reality.

The Miraculous Ones and the Prodigies are now going to return in great numbers and through the use of *force*. And that is just as true as the fact that I was Born in Marseille on 4 September 1896 at 8 o'clock in the morning.

You haven't been able to find your place in the Political World because the Political World is the domain of men, and you are an Inspired One, and Men have never wanted Inspired Ones among them.

Your rightful place will be in making war against the Political World and you are going to become the *leader* of a Movement of warfare against all of the Human *factions*. Because you've had as much as you can take of Human factions. You are above all of that. And *I have always been able to see* you as being above all of that, and that's why I have always found it unbearable to see you subjugate yourself – you, Breton – to factions, to rules and to Human categories which manifest themselves in Systems, Doctrines and Political Parties.

That's what I've been wanting to say to you for more than 10 years now.

A process of liquefaction will soon have taken hold of *all* of those parties and *all of the men* and will have transformed all of those currently in power into nullities, and it's then that Your Hour will come. And if today you are feeling discouraged, pushed-aside, stamped-upon, trampled-upon, and you are feeling desperate, my dear friend, I know you are going to be able to rediscover your life's force, your courage, your Momentum, your daring, and your AUTHORITY.

You are not going to be able to get frightened when it will be time to propel yourself into the Crowd, in confrontation with Men, and to demand recognition of your Truth, which is the Truth.

I am not going to be in France at the moment when that happens, but I will be back there soon, and the face of this country where I am now will *also* be changed and I am going to set out for other countries.

I embrace you.

ANTONIN ARTAUD

P.S. – I've changed my address. I left the Aran Islands and I am going to leave for another part of Ireland.

You can write to me at:

Mail General Delivery – Central
Galway
Ireland.

[Notes: Artaud wrote this letter on headed paper of the Imperial Hotel, Galway, but crossed out the hotel's name and address. The woman Artaud refers to is the writer and arts promoter Lise Deharme, for whom Artaud developed a deep antipathy in the period before his departure for Ireland, since he believed she had ridiculed him. Théroigne de Mericourt was a hero of the French Revolution; she was initially lauded but then beaten and incarcerated in an insane asylum. The long-term involvement with the French Communist Party of André Breton and the Surrealist movement had ended in acrimony in 1935.]

To Jean Paulhan,

2 September or 3 September 1937

(Letter, sent from Galway)

Dear friend,

For some time now, I've been making many sacrifices.

I am hoping that you are going to be able to send
me the few hundred francs which I need here. Gaston Gallimard, who wasn't afraid to demand that I
accept a cut of 3% in my royalties, now really *has
to* give me at least the same *advance* sum which
he gives to others, 1,500 francs in all, for the com-
pleted book which he's had already for 2 years. I've
had 700 francs, so 800 remain, and I need that sum
here and I hope it will not be refused to me and *that
it will be sent to me urgently.* You have supported
and helped me with the heart of a friend, so you
will understand my utter exasperation in the face
of the downfall of everything I have tried to do for
too many years now. Jean Paulhan, please, do what
has to be done.

I've changed my address here. You need to send the
money to

MAIL GENERAL DELIVERY – Central
at
GALWAY
IRELAND

I am counting on you to do this without fail. IT IS VERY URGENT!!!

Fondly yours,

ANTONIN ARTAUD.

[Notes: As with the previous letter, Artaud wrote this letter on headed paper of the Imperial Hotel, Galway, and again crossed out the hotel's name and address. Gaston Gallimard was one of Artaud's publishers. The book Artaud refers to as awaiting publication is *The Theatre and its Double*; it was eventually published in the following year.]

To André Breton, 5 September 1937

(LETTER WITH AN ACCOMPANYING MAGIC SPELL,
SENT FROM GALWAY)

Dear friend,

I am entrusting to you a Magic Spell that I'm sending to Madame X. If she sees my handwriting, she may well not open the envelope. So write the address in a style that doesn't look like mine. And do send it to her, I beg of you.

You are going to see, once you have examined the Magic Spell, that things are about to become serious and that this time, I'm going to the very end of everything.

Madame X.'s grave responsibility lies in having said that there are no more Gods. That's the reason for my hatred of her.

Because there are still Gods, even though God no longer exists. And ranged above gods there is the unconscious, criminal law of Nature, and the gods and Us – that is, *We the Gods* – are collectively victims of that law.

Paganism had everything right, but Men – who are always utter bastards – betrayed the Pagan Truth. So christ has returned in order to illuminate the Pagan Truth, which *all* the various christian Churches have been shitting on in an ignominious way. This christ I'm talking about was a Magician who fought with Demons in the desert, using a cane as his weapon. And a trace of his blood remained imprinted on that cane. That trace disappears when you wipe it away with water, *but then it comes back.*

Within certain Men there is a god who is coming back, and those men struggle against that god, because he exhausts them *in a material way.* But gods always impose themselves in the end.

These gods can never seize power because they never impose themselves – in taking control of space, or by their nature – except to destroy all power.

You need to listen to the Pagan Truth. There is no God, but gods still exist. At the summit of the gods' Hierarchy there's the greatest God that Plato speaks about, who like everything else that exists is Nature's victim. That greatest God isn't a criminal, but a Powerless One, like Us. It's Nature that is criminal – and what is Nature exactly? In itself, it's Nothingness. It is that Nothingness that Lao-Tzu talks about, but even so, Life itself issues from that Nothingness.

What does that mean?

It means that it's impossible to conceive that what is, really isn't, and that nothing exists. To think that through is an *essential* absurdity. Every law wants to make it believed that something exists. *But our work is to destroy the Law.*

Any revolt of Black magicians against God is only an act of weakness and an absurdity. Because there are no gods, but there is yourself, and when you yourself rise up against this so-called God then you are also rising up against yourself, and it's your own downfall that you are creating for yourself.

Anaximander, the Initiate of the School of Ionia, said this:

'Beings emerge from the Infinite and they will return to it, according to *a necessary law*, because they need to be punished and to expiate their injustice towards one another, according to the law of things.'

The force of the law expelled those beings, and set them outside, into life. They left the infinity of Nothingness because whatever becomes something is no longer the Infinite. But Beings have always formed a triangle with Mankind and Infinity. And the Gods too have always formed triangles and they move towards the Infinite which keeps eating them up, again and again, because the Infinite is the enemy of gods, as it is the enemy of God. This infinite, this Nothingness, is the Hindu state of Non-Being. And between Mankind and the primordial Non-Being, we are this Non-Being and these Gods, positioned within an immense hierarchy of gods.

Life was never given to us and we were never induced to enter Life, because it's we ourselves who created Life with the sole aim of *punishing within ourselves* this criminal force of Being which ceaselessly harasses us.

Anyone who flees from life thereby loses the benefits to be gained from the destruction of the Law, and so becomes subjugated once again to the blows of the Law. And we really have to destroy the law. Because the only secret in life is that of learning how to destroy the law in order to fall once again into a state of Non-Being *above Eternity itself.*

And THAT ITSELF IS THE LAW.

Because Eternity will never give you any rest. And this Law will allow you to return to a state of rest, above the possible and the impossible, and above all Eternities.

The principle of contradiction is integral to the very nature of being, and you have to kill even that state of being in order to escape from contradiction.

To be within life, while at the same time refusing life – I'm speaking about someone who understood how to be able to bear life only by forbidding himself the joys of life. He has earned his rest and he is never coming back, because he has succeeded in being able to *remain* in Non-Being – and even if criminal Nature itself reappears because it can give itself no peace, he himself will never reappear in Nature, and he will escape from the Hierarchy of the gods. He is neither the First god, nor the last man – he is going to stay in irreality.

And there's as much danger to risk in being the First God as there is in risking being the last Man, and there are as many First Gods as there are Eternities, and there will always be a first god and a last man. What is important is to escape from this circle which never ceases to start up again.

All of this isn't a theory – it's the Truth. It's the Truth as I've seen it and that I can translate, in as much as these matters can be translated. Whoever doesn't want to understand this Truth, I'm going to smash them in the face this time. Because this Truth is going to have to be imposed by force. For everyone's good. And people may not understand the force of truth, but they certainly will understand the truth of the violent force which will then make them accept – wholeheartedly and in all consciousness – the force of truth. I'll be starting on this work two months from now.

I am against the Jews only to the extent that they have renounced the Kabbalah – all of the Jews who have not renounced the Kabbalah are with me – but the others: No.

It's likely that I am going to be put into Prison some time from now. You don't need to worry, it will be intentional on my part and will be only for a short time.

I have told you before that I once read in the Tarot cards that I was going to have to get into a fight against justice but that I didn't know if justice was going to beat me down to a pulp or if it was going to be me who beat down justice.

It's me who is going to beat down justice.

Your friend.

I'm signing here for one of the last times with my own Name, and after that I will have another Name.

ANTONIN ARTAUD.

[Artaud's 'Magic Spell' was enclosed within this letter to André Breton, but was contained in a separate envelope with the imprint of the Imperial Hotel, Galway; it was written in black ink on one sheet of paper, and burned in its centre, probably with a cigarette.]

5 September 1937

5   9   2

14   2

7

7

I am going to shove
a cross of iron
reddened by fire into your
stinking Jew's cunt
and then perform some *bad acting*
over your dead body in order to
prove to you that
GODS STILL EXIST!

[Notes: André Breton did not pass on Artaud's 'Magic Spell' to Lise Deharme, and instead kept it. The spell's date is given in a form partly devised from kabbalistic calculations. Artaud was himself part-Jewish, on his mother's side.]

Anne.

It's certain that in Paris, there's an intention to get me arrested.

You mustn't worry about this.

A *rich* woman – whom I had charitably warned to leave behind her involvement with communism since otherwise she would herself have to take the blame for risking being caught up in the coming massacre of an insurrection of the forces of the left – replied to me that she would have me burned as a sorcerer. And that I was a wretchedly bad actor. She told me, moreover, that she wanted to eat alive all those who still speak of God. I then replied in specifying to her the torture that would be imposed upon her for her revolt – the torture that would take place *after* the massacre which she herself is instigating – and I told her that, in accordance with the Justice of God – I would then perform some bad acting over her dead body on that day.

[Note: On the back of the two torn pieces of paper, Artaud wrote fragments of another text, which may have been intended for incorporation into a letter which was either abandoned or is now lost: 'The Man has been able to see that Ireland hasn't betrayed him,/God is everything/but everything is not God,/this language that a French person can no longer understand was at the origin of a right which the ancient high Kings of Ireland held, to rule while disdaining to govern./the Kings of England betrayed that language.']

To André Breton, 8 September 1937

(Letter, sent from Galway)

My very dear friend,

You are going to have to tell Mme X. that if she has the plan to come looking for me in Ireland, she would do well to save herself the trip. She is not going to find me! On the other hand, I am going to be able to find her, when the right time comes. She shouldn't feel too triumphant if she discovers herself still alive on the 1st of January 1938. A temporary reprieve can certainly be accorded to her. In order that she can leave behind that which she has been told to leave behind.

In any case, all those who claim to only want to believe in what they can see – those like that Rich, Sinister woman, that sinister daughter of the Jewish Bankers who created the Modern World, and who claim that there is no God – will soon understand that it's God alone responsible when they see the strangling of the Modern World. I am going to reinstate the idea of the Eternal God in everyone's consciousness, in the dead centre of the splitting-apart of all consciousnesses.

And this will be the Truth.

I am leaving Galway now and I am going towards my Destiny.

Antonin Artaud.
8 September 1937.

I am counting on you to send that Magic Spell.

[Note: Artaud wrote this letter on headed paper of the Imperial Hotel, Galway, but crossed out the hotel's name and address.]

My life on earth is what it has to be: that's to say, riven with insurmountable difficulties that I have to surmount. Because that's the Law.

But I'm noticing now that you *do not want to understand me*. And evidently, there is nothing to be done about this. For you, I'm some kind of great spectacle, but you're not getting into the game. You perhaps regard my existence as a form of brilliant proposition, somehow positioned outside of this world – and you believe yourself, you, to be within the World – but you're not able to see that the World is now in the process of cracking-apart under your feet, and you're not able to see that it's for you that I'm working, if you can understand that. The Truth, dear Anne – *and you really have to let this inside your head* – is that in 1 year's time, and happening simultaneously at that time, everything you see and everything that constitutes your life in that world, WILL HAVE BLOWN APART – listen to me – and you will *NO LONGER BE ABLE EVEN TO RECOGNISE YOURSELF* if you continue in this way.

It's You, not Me, who is living in a state of illusion and blindness. You're certainly right that I'm suffering, but that will only subsist for a short time, because in my current exhausted life I'm in the process of preparing something which is not some kind of daydream, but an Advanced Calculation, of a kind that the current Era has become too stupid to understand – and that's why nothing will remain of it in only a few months' time:

A prophecy written-down 14 centuries ago, and which has been published, and which I've VERIFIED point by point *in* all of its F A C T S over the last months, announces a horrendous future for the World.

This future is now very near.

A large part of Paris will shortly be engulfed by fire and will disappear. Nothing will be spared that city and that country – earthquakes, plague, insurrections and bursts of gunfire in the streets. This is as certain as that It's certain that I was born on the 4th of September 1896 at 8 o'clock in the morning, in Marseille, and it's as certain as the fact that you are not hesitating to get involved in dealings with detestable newspapers in order to write articles on detestable subject matters. By doing that, you are compromising the marvellous light that is inside of you and which gives you your grandeur – but it's a grandeur that is now often eclipsed and a light that's hidden under a bushel.

I am writing to you in this way because I *want* to have a high conception of you. You're thinking too much of the details of your own particular life and not enough about another life – *which is becoming more and more vitally relevant for you* – but which I'm afraid that you are not going to be able to understand except through catastrophe, just like everyone else. And that makes me despair. It's futile to complain about your sufferings with tennis games, with going fishing, with your family, with how hot it is, and about not being in Mexico – when all you got out of going to Mexico was a kind of egotistical sensuality, individualised in a horrendous way – and when modern life is made up exclusively of those starving to death and without any family, of the mad, of maniacs, of imbeciles and of those made desperate by the errors of modern life.

What the Anarchists in Spain are doing is very daring, but at the same time it's a human aberration. These maps of love and bread are the consecration of an *inhuman* disorder.

Because what people call *human* today is the castration of a person's superhuman dimension.

It's an error in the absolute.

The Anarchists in Spain are attempting in a *catastrophic* way to fix the absolute of life in the world. That's a lie and it's a dishonest idea. That idea is *not* itself any kind of *force driven by love*. Because what is the priority of an anarchist? To fix in this world the *property of the self.*

Anarchists are detestable, pleasure-obsessed proprietors.

All they deserve is to be massacred. And they are going to be. Because they're using Lies! You just can't deal with all of the embodiments of the Lie. Instead you need to destroy them all, in order to bring to light The Man with the Truth, the Man with Love, I mean with the Love of Truth!

Despite all that, you are still able to have some strange divinations concerning me!

ANTONIN ARTAUD.

I am leaving Galway now
But even so, write to me

Mail General Delivery
at *Galway*,

and they'll forward on your letters.

Don't give my address to *Anybody* in Paris. This is very important.

[Note: Anne Manson had apparently written to Artaud that she would soon be travelling to Spain to report as a journalist on the Anarchist forces engaged in the Spanish Civil War (at a point of particularly fierce fighting between the war's factions in September 1937), and parts of Artaud's letter evidently respond directly to that (lost) letter's news, as well as intimating his unhappiness that she would be absent from Paris.]

To Anne Manson, 13 September 1937

(Letter, partly lost, sent from Dublin)

13 September 1937.

My dear Anne, Your much-appreciated attitude towards me now leads me to make a certain number of highly significant revelations to you. And you will *have to* believe what I tell you, because I swear to you that it's not through my own inclination that I am now submitting myself to the orders of God. Propelled by colossal forces, I have finally discovered *who* I have been and have accepted who I have been. Every day, the Voice of christ is revealing to me the doctrine of life and of death, along with the mystery of birth and the mystery of the Incarnations. I now know – *unfortunately* – I now know how this world was created and I have been assigned the *Mission* to reveal this to all of the World, and it's an amazing and terrifying Mystery to be the one to say that christ is the Prince of the Destruction of all things and that he has come here to stand with those who have been able to see the evil of Life. Through his pity for human beings and his hatred for the horrendous suffering involved in being alive, he wanted to be able to teach to them the secret of detachment from this world, and the way to return to the disappearance of Life. The christ-Shiva is the Negative of Creation. It's he who says *no* to life, through hatred of life, but...

[Here two pages of the letter have been lost.]

[...]

God himself to enter battle, with the forces of christ-Shiva himself, with forces – themselves immense – of Vishnu the Holy-Spirit, Krishna.

Because the Son, christ and Shiva are the same thing,

The Holy-Spirit, Vishnu and Krishna are also the same thing.

It's not a force of hatred that christ wants to extend over the world's surface, but a colossal force of love. This force will direct itself to the hearts of human beings and instruct them about the void of life and what is sublime about the disappearance of forms. Mankind will resist christ and will want to kill the man who is the representative of this force. As a result, this force will manifest itself in all of its force, and in its cruelty, but solely in order to have done with that resistance of mankind. Because cruelty is not some kind of luxury, Anne – so don't be stupid and sentimental at the same time as you are sublime. *To be cruel, you have to have become illuminated.* That's the truth. I'm warning you: Just don't play games with me. Cruelty is not some kind of game, and I do not love it. But I will impose cruelty when I have to. I embrace you.

ANTONIN ARTAUD.

If you yourself are going to become cruel, that would be aimed *against* yourself. No being is going to be able to get hold of the one to whom God is now talking, on a daily basis – UNFORTUNATELY. And I swear that the cruelty of God is something to which you will never attain. ------------- Anne!

Send me, by telegraphic means, that which you are offering me and which I asked you for, because it COULD BE too late for me without that.

Do it, *for the best.*

Anne,
by telegraphic means,
for the Sign.

[Notes: Only the first and last of the letter's four pages have survived. On the last of the sheets of paper used for this letter, Artaud had previously written a message in English to reassure the lighthouse keeper who rented him a room in his house in Eoghanacht on the island of Inishmore, at the moment when Artaud left Inishmore to travel to Galway: 'I go to Galway *with the priest* to take money in Post office.' At the end of the letter, Artaud is asking Anne Manson to send him a sum of money by telegraphic transfer.]

I now have to reveal to you, Anne, that in a few days (Around 20) I will be speaking publicly In The Name of God himself,

because there is a secret to my Life and in my Birth, Anne.

I will be speaking in the Name of the 2nd State of the Universal Manifestation,

the State of the Destruction of forms, and for the transformation of forms and for the Sublime in them, that means speaking for the State of the disappearance of Being, and of the Return to the absolute of All Beings, which is known by Brahmanistic Hindus as Shiva and who is incarnated in the person of christ himself ! ! !

I am going to be preaching about the return of christ as he appeared in the catacombs, and that will bring about the return of the christian-ism of the catacombs. The visible forms of catholicism will then be razed on account of its idolatry, and the current Pope is going to be condemned to death as a traitor, and for the crime of simony.

If all of that makes you feel panic-stricken, just keep in mind my hatred of human flesh. I am writing this to you with the sole aim that you will now follow me. Come and rejoin me in Ireland in the month of October – but I swear to you that by then, nobody will be concerned any longer with the war in Spain nor with battles in the Mediterranean.

I have hold of the *Cane* of Jesus-christ and it's Jesus-christ who is giving me orders about everything that I am going to undertake, and you will see that his

Teaching was intended for the benefit of Metaphysical Heroes and not for idiots.

You are a heroine, Anne, and I embrace you. *But above life.*

ARTAUD.

REPLY TO ME IMMEDIATELY.

My dear Annie, My dear Thomas,

If anyone comes to 21 Rue Daguerre, and asks if I'm married,
    of course, *reply No*,
    but if you are asked *if there was ever any question of me getting married*,
    you then also have to Reply *No, that I never even thought about it.*
    Listen to me: my existence, my very *EXISTENCE*, hangs on your reply.
    I can't tell you now what this is all about, but it's a matter of the utmost gravity.
    The truth is that in this World, there are immense mysteries, and that the World is not what everyone believes it to be, and that it is especially not as it is seen by those who say that they believe only what they can see.
    My dear Annie, my dear Thomas, the truth is that I have entered into the mysteries of the World through the *cane of Jesus-christ* which my friend René Thomas gave to me. Because the cane I hold is that of Jesus-christ,
    and the two of you, who know full well that I am not mad, you are going to believe me when I tell you that Jesus-christ is talking to me now every day and is *revealing to me everything* that is going to happen, and is giving me orders to do what I am going to do.

I therefore came here to Ireland to obey the orders of God, the Son, incarnated in Jesus-christ.

It was through the intervention of Jesus-christ that Marie-Anne left this cane at 21 Rue Daguerre, with Thomas, so that Thomas would give it to me and that the cane would be able to do its special work.

It's because the cane spent time at Rue Daguerre that all of the Beings who have played a crucial role in my life have themselves passed through the Rue Daguerre.

My dear friends, in around 20 days from now – and I say this without any kind of boasting, because my acts are propelled solely by God and without Him I would not act at all – in around 20 days from now you will hear a great thundercrack resound over the World, because the cane of Jesus-christ will be instrumental in the End of the World and it will need to battle against the antichrist. The antichrist himself will not arrive for several years yet, but in 20 days the face of all things is going to be changed and nobody will care anymore about the war in China, or about battles in the Mediterranean. I swear to you that England will have something entirely different to contend with, because it's going to disappear from the face of the map, and part of the Island of England *is going to disappear underneath the sea*.

If I was only a man, I would say that I am going to be in deadly danger, but there exists within me someone else who gives me warnings of what is going to have to happen and who tells me I have nothing to fear. Just know this – and it's all I can tell you for the moment: 20 days from now I will be speaking in the Name of God Himself, at the centre of a burst of thunder sent by God.

Unfortunately I will not be taking any glory from this myself, because soon I will no longer be calling myself Antonin Artaud, I am going to become an other, and the Duty weighing on me is terrifying. Annie, it's terrifying to discover so suddenly the truth of *who* you are and that, in reality, you were an other – and this other was Rameses II in Egypt – *really*, Annie, *really* – and that you have also been other people over the course of time, all of them charged with terrible responsibilities by some form of power or other, itself also terrible, perhaps, but also crushing.

I can tell you as well that I now know that demons exist, because I have seen them and heard them,

I know also that a plot...

[Notes: The end of the letter is lost. Artaud oscillated between spelling Anie Besnard's first name as 'Anie' and 'Annie'. Artaud stayed at René Thomas's apartment at 21 Rue Daguerre in the Montparnasse district of Paris before his departure for Ireland. His preoccupation with marriage plans may relate to his broken-off marriage plans with Cécile Schramme from the Spring of 1937.]

To André Breton, 14 September 1937

(Letter, sent by Artaud from Dublin to
Anne Manson, to send on from Paris to Breton]

14 September 1937.

My dear Breton, My Friend,

A huge sorrow for me – certainly the greatest of all those sorrows which I am now still able to feel – is that you are separating yourself from me and that you are no longer following me in my new and *last* vision. This sorrow isn't caused by me – *it's caused by you yourself,* and this time the wrong you are doing is *irreparable.*

During the course of my abominable existence, I've had occasion to abandon very many things – in the end, I've abandoned everything – right down to the very idea of Existence. And it was while I was searching for INEXISTENCE that I rediscovered what God is. So if I'm talking about God, it's not to live, but to die.

It wasn't God who created Human Beings, instead it was Human Beings who created God, thereby polluting their chance of being able to escape from the human – that is, from *the state which makes you suffer the most.* Human Beings are at the origin of suffering and not God.

It's the human state which defiles, which pollutes, which diminishes and which is *relentlessly* ridiculing what is now the anachronistic force of God.

That force of God didn't create human beings in the way that those eternally idiotic Human Beings understand it, but it *made human beings* ALSO *in the way that they should be made*. That is, so that they would display the expanse of the possible and of the impossible, about which that force of God has always dreamed.

It so happens that among the manifestations of that force of God there is what the Hindus call the Triad of Brahma, Shiva and Vishnu – what we call the Trinity of the Holy Father, the Son and the Holy Spirit – but in reality the Son-Shiva works AGAINST the MANIFESTATION OF CREATION by the HOLY FATHER, which is MAINTAINED by the Holy Spirit. Because the Son-Shiva also possesses Force, but it's the Force of Transmutation, that's to say the *destruction* of all forms, that's to say the passage *into* and *through* all forms, without ever stopping on any one of them, so that force is the very force of the Absolute. Those who are searching for the absolute are allied with the Son, against the Father, and ABOVE ALL against the Holy Spirit.

Because it's the Holy Spirit, the hideous dove (the Dove YONAH, and YONI the vagina) which imposes the duration of life, as one among life's delightful contradictions.

The Holy Father isn't the first God, but he represents the FIRST AWARENESS of the horrible Force of Nature which is what creates BEING, and thereby brings about the calamity which all BEINGS endure.

The Force of *Nature* is the Law, and that Law is the *Nature of things* which in all cases makes the Law, whether you accept or reject the Law. And it's We, too, who made the Law and are the Law – whether the officials and accomplices of the Law want it or not.

THAT'S THE WAY IT IS and THERE IS Nothing TO BE DONE ABOUT IT.

To deny it is to deny ourselves. To the extent that you don't understand that, you understand nothing of life or of the disorder of life or of how to bring *resolution* to the evil of life.

You can't rebel against the Law, but you can rebel against criminal disorder and against the consequences of the Law.

But for that you need a Science. To combat the disorder of God you need what is currently called a technique.

And it was to reveal to us that technique that the rebellious Son came to us, against his Father – and to do that, he took the form of christ.

And the true christ is the one who gave me his own cane, his magical and irresistible stick, and I beg you to believe that this has got nothing to do with christianity's christ nor with catholicism's christ.

Now, just listen to this.

We ourselves are the force of life, but that force is not eternal, whether or not it's called the Breath of God, the Ain Soph which the Kabbalah speaks about – whatever breathes is not eternal – and even God's Breath has only a fixed duration.

As long as that life force is in existence, the Eternal Triad – which made Beings appear – then destroys them in order to sublimate them through the Son-Shiva before recomposing them through the sustaining force of the Holy Spirit-Vishnu.

All of these forces remain in equivalence for long periods of time, but a time comes when they all destroy one another and then reunite in order to die.

The moment has now come when they must all die. And that's the explanation for the current disorder of these Times.

Yes, my dear Breton, those Times have come, as announced by the apocalypse in which christ – in order to punish his Church – engages an Enraged One who will raze EVERY Church and dispatch the rites of the INITIATED below the earth.

The current Pope is going to be condemned to death by this ENRAGED ONE to whom the true christ is speaking – and he is speaking to him every single day.

This christ, Jesus-christ, was a man like you and me. And I swear to you that he laughed darkly about the hideousness of his so-called Name and about the Images that were called his images. And he laughed – as much as it's possible to laugh about it – about religious rituals and the *external* paraphernalia of religious worship, because this man – in whom the second Time, the Son Shiva of the Eternal Manifestation was incarnated – was a fearsome Initiate whom Mankind afterwards caricatured. He was the negative force of Nature – that is, he was the force which had seen the evil of life and called for the Merit of Dying. And if he wanted to pass through a corporeal form, it was in order to teach us to destroy bodies, and to push away all attachment to bodies.

It's the Holy Spirit which preserves bodies and makes us want to believe in the fact of being alive, and it's the Holy Spirit which denies the Absolute. And it's the Son who brings things back to the absolute. Vishnu the Holy Spirit was incarnated in another era in India, and that is why the Hindus of the Vedas say that they too possess the Incarnation of a God – but that isn't the same God.

Let me say it again: For as long as the force of manifestation is living, then Brahma, Shiva and Vishnu are in a state of equilibrium and the World is living a kind of golden age, but a time arrives when that force of life must die. This time has now come, and so the Time has come when the Son and the Holy Spirit are going to enter into conflict and destroy one another in order to engender the disappearance of everything which exists.

Because if the Son Shiva – the christ – is going to engage an Enraged One to exert the downfall of christ's ridiculous Church, then the Holy Spirit Vishnu Krishna is going to engage the antichrist. Yes – it's the Holy Spirit itself which is going to engage the antichrist. I know that sounds utterly unbelievable.

And just as the Enraged One exists, the antichrist also exists, today, and you yourself, Breton, you know the antichrist. Because, André Breton, this is what you are going to have to understand: It's the *Unbelievable* – yes, the Unbelievable – it's the Unbelievable which is the truth.

You personally know the one who is going to become the antichrist – you have shaken his hand – he is younger than I am and he loves Life just as much as I hate it.

This idea is going to appear outlandish to you, but the antichrist is a regular at the Deux Magots café. And another prominent figure involved in the coming apocalypse has also been seen around at the Deux Magots.

This is how it is and I swear that I am not joking. *Where* I am now, I hardly want to joke.

Jesus-christ – in the figure of a man – has arrived in order to instigate, in the domain of the spirit, a rite of the disappearance of things, employing the same principle as that of Human sacrifices. Only imbeciles would understand all that as just consisting of massacre, assassination and Suicide. It actually consists – since we are alive – of living while refusing life, of perceiving things in such a way that they rise up and not in such a way that they flatten themselves on the ground, and of perceiving things in such a way that they will disappear and not in such a way that they will fix themselves within reality. Because in the true doctrine of christ, the Holy Spirit is a Bourgeois who is stuck in one place while christ is the never-ending Revolutionary. The 2nd force of God, Shiva, is the revolutionary, and the 3rd force of God, Vishnu, is reactionary.

Now you have to choose!

The rite instigated by christ is a rite of revolutionary High Magic, from which these eternal Bourgeois priest-Men, who are fixed in one place, then invented the catholic Mass ritual which gives me Nausea.

In that rite of christ, Human Beings eat the flesh of a Man who *wanted* to sacrifice himself to the point of death, and they thereby eat their own disappearance and confirm their contempt for the duration of things, for things' *artificiality* and for all effigies of things.

If that rite isn't transcendent in its immediate and real manifestation, then *it doesn't exist*.

That rite is a kind of essential theatre, and even in the secret temples of India where Brahmanism possesses no rituals, it still possesses rites of an essential theatre.

Because even in order to affirm that we want nothing of the state of Being, we still need to make use of beings, that's to say: to make use of what has been created. It's necessary to have contact with renounced objects in order to invite them to destroy themselves with us, at the same time as us. The rite of christ takes elements of a renounced world and it invites them to disappear, but only after *inviting them to take a good look at themselves*.

You can only effectively renounce something by doing it in a material way.

So I am going to call together the Black Magicians – those who renounce God in order better to destroy him and who are in a state of insurrection against the Force of God which compelled them to exist. And I am going to say to them: Your own Hatred is justified but it's badly directed. – You have a means to avenge yourself against God, this God who compelled you to exist and who created the evil of existence. It's in your Human brains that you rose up against God, but Human Beings can do nothing against God – only God can do something against God. The God who is compelling you to exist is the 3rd force-God – the one named Vishnu by Hindus, and the Holy Spirit by christians. You need instead to think about God from within the brain of God, and rise up against the Holy Spirit, and the Son-Shiva-christ stands with you against the Holy Spirit. – So the days of the Holy Spirit are numbered because we're arrived at the end of the world. The 3 forces of God which used to be in equilibrium are now going to destroy one another, and in order to destroy one another they are going to enter into a state of warfare, one against the other, and devour one another.

And this is going to be war, all of this is going to be the war of the Son against the Holy Spirit and of christ against the antichrist. With these two immense forces of Nature entering into their struggle, you need to understand the importance of that struggle and the terrible stakes of that struggle, but above all you need to understand the fearsome Power of the antichrist supported by the Holy Spirit. It's because the force of life is at its end that the antichrist – who represents life and the attachment to the appearances of life – will be destroyed, but not before he directly or indirectly destroys many things and many people. So it will be catastrophic for those who join the side of the antichrist, who is upholding life and the pleasures of life – when Life itself is now evidently falling into a state of rottenness – yes, it will be catastrophic for those who oppose the Enraged One who is going to invite human beings to no longer live and to discover that it's better to die. – Because it's more intelligent to follow the true course of things, rather than to rise up against the course of things.

If you believe all of this, then I have the right to tell you that a fearsome form of power will be placed at your service and at the service of everything which you have ever believed to be beautiful, to be just, to be great, to be *unbelievable*, and to be desperate.

If you do not believe all of this, then I will have to search for another just man.

But until now, you are the most just Man that I have ever encountered.

I embrace you.

ART.

[Notes: Artaud sent this letter to Anne Manson in Paris in order for her to mail it on to Breton from there, possibly because of Artaud's great preoccupation with secrecy. The Deux Magots is a well-known café in Paris, and one frequently visited by Artaud. It's not known which two regulars of the Deux Magots Artaud had in mind in notifying Breton of the location of the Antichrist and of the other figure he saw as being closely involved in the coming Apocalypse.]

(Letter, partly lost, sent from Dublin)

Get going to the Deux Magots, Woman, *betray me*. Tell them there that I'm in Dublin so that they can come and capture me.

But warn them too that they are going to get what is coming to them. And it will be unstoppable and WITHOUT Mercy.

They need to know that I will not be coming back alone, but will have an army with me. If they believe me to be mad, megalomaniacal or maniacal, so much the worse for them. And if they believe that I am boasting, then they are imbeciles.

Just tell them that for years now I've hated them, all of them and their political, social, moral, amoral and immoral ideas. Tell them that I consider them to be scoundrels and a set of cunts.

Just tell them that I shit on the republic, on democracy, on socialism, on communism, on Marxism, on idealism, on materialism – whether it's dialectical materialism or not, because I shit on dialectics too, and I'm going to give you further proof of that.

I shit on the Popular Front and I shit on the Government of the Popular Alliance, I shit on the International Workingmen's Association, in its 1st, 2nd and 3rd variants, but I also shit on the idea of a National Homeland, I shit on France and on *every last one* of the French – with the exception of those to whom I've personally issued warnings from here in Ireland and those with whom I'm in correspondence.

The French – whether they believe themselves to be on the Right or on the Left – are all a bunch of cunts who want to own things, and in that stinking café to which I'm now sending you – where they all exhausted and exasperated me with their quarrels and their little self-interests – I never saw anyone except people who wanted to own things, *people stuck in one place*, stuck, petrified to the point of blindness by existence, and *every one of them* has spread their darkness over Existence. To the point of being driven crazy, I have had ENOUGH of them. Just tell them that, for me, there are no men of the left, but...

[Note: The end of the letter is lost.]

To Jacqueline Breton,

17 September 1937

(Magic Spell, sent from Dublin)

17 – 9 – 2

I will send a Magic Spell
to the First One who dares to touch you.
I am going to beat
his little gob of a fake proud cock
to a *pulp*.
I am going to flay his arse in front of 100,000 people !
HIS PAINTING WHICH WAS
NEVER VERY
STRIKING HAS NOW BECOME
DEFINITIVELY
 BAD
HIS VOICE IS TOO UGLY

IT'S THE ANTICHRIST

[Notes: This protective 'Magic Spell' was sent directly to Jacqueline Breton, as opposed to the hostile spell sent indirectly to Lise Deharme, via André Breton (who kept it). The spell's date is given in a form partly devised from kabbalistic calculations. The phrase 'IT'S THE ANTICHRIST' is underlined five times. It's not known which painter Artaud had in mind as the Antichrist.]

To Jacqueline Breton,

21 September 1937

(Letter, sent from Dublin)

You will be *Avenged*, my dear Jacqueline, as will the Superior Being for whom *you are* the Predestined Spouse.

You are a Noble heart, a courageous Spirit, a generous soul.

You consider yourself to be bad, and you are mistaken, it's your imagination which creates in you the false idea of wickedness with a pure exterior, it's not your Nature.

I am going to reveal to your Husband a number of Mysteries, and also what a sublime Position he occupies in the order of the Spirits who are the creators of this World.

He is the active intelligence of Brahma, the Father, who was represented in the Symbolism of the Middle Ages by the *Angel Gabriel*.

This was the Spirit who made visible Nature *appear*, as well as the 4 Elements.

21 September 1937.

I am sending a Magic Spell *to Sonia*.

[Notes: Artaud wrote the letter's date and the note about sending a 'Magic Spell' (which is lost) to his friend Sonia Mossé on the letter's envelope, the date on the front and the note on the back. The envelope is stamped 6.05pm on 21 September 1937. This was the last of Artaud's letters from Ireland to have survived; he was deported eight days later, on 29 September.]

Notes on Artaud's correspondents

René Thomas was an artist who had helped Artaud in his period of near-destitution in Paris immediately prior to his departure for Ireland.

André Breton was the leader of the Surrealist movement, and temporarily on friendly terms with Artaud in 1937 after a long period of mutual hostility. They did not meet again until 1946, after Artaud's asylum incarceration.

Anne Manson was a Paris-based journalist specialising in the subject of Mexico, where Artaud travelled, especially to the Tarahumara lands, in 1936. 'Anne Manson' was a pseudonym; her real name was Georgette Dunais.

Jean Paulhan was a prominent literary editor and publisher, best known in 1937 as editor of the journal *La Nouvelle Revue Française*.

Lise Deharme was a writer and a prolific promoter of Surrealist and other arts events; she had infuriated Artaud by (as he saw it) denigrating him and his work, shortly before his departure for Ireland.

Anie Besnard was a close friend of Artaud from an early age; he wrote frequently to her from his subsequent asylum incarceration, and received visits from her, but believed she had been killed and replaced by a double.

Jacqueline Breton (better known as Jacqueline Lamba) was an artist, designer and dancer, and the wife of André Breton from 1934 to 1943.

NOTES ON THE TRANSLATIONS

The New Revelations of Being (*Les Nouvelles Révélations de l'Être*) is an Apocalypse manifesto, partly in the form of a tarot reading, which Artaud wrote in Paris in June 1937. It was published as a small, anonymous booklet in July 1937. Only the untitled short prelude (originally printed on the inside of the front cover) and the untitled preface are translated here. I have used the original edition of 1937.

Artaud's editor Paule Thévenin collected all of his surviving letters, postcards and magic spells written from Ireland from their recipients and published them in 1970 in volume VII of Artaud's *Œuvres complètes*. This is the edition I have used. I was able to view several of the original letters from Ireland in Paule Thévenin's personal collection, prior to her death in 1993, as well as letters and magic spells preserved in other collections and archives, such as the Bibliothèque Jacques Doucet in Paris. Some of Artaud's letters were certainly lost, either at the time of his journey in 1937 or over subsequent decades, notably at least one of the letters which he wrote to Anne Manson from Dublin, and also the magic spell which he mentions sending to Sonia Mossé in his letter to Jacqueline Breton of 21 September 1937. No letters sent by Artaud's correspondents to him in Ireland appear to have survived.

AFTERWORD

STEPHEN BARBER

Artaud's journey from Paris to Ireland in August to September 1937 is a profound mystery. There is no rational explanation why he made the journey, other than that he went there in order to witness signs of the oncoming Apocalypse. In the manifesto text, *The New Revelations of Being*, which he wrote in June 1937, during a period of near-destitution in Paris following his return from an arduous journey to Mexico to visit the Tarahumara lands and to attempt to take peyote, and which was published anonymously in the following month as a small booklet of orange card imprinted with red and black lettering, containing densely printed pages, Artaud had specified '7 November 1937' as the day when 'Destruction' – after several months of escalating fulmination and the illumination of ominous signs – finally 'bursts into lightning', with the result that: 'the Tortured One [Artaud himself] has become for everyone the Recognised One,/THE REVEALED ONE.'

From the port of Cobh in County Cork, Artaud travelled to Inishmore, one of the three Aran islands. Although he carried a cane which he identified as having belonged to Saint Patrick, and whose historical counterpart, the 'Bachal Isu', had been preserved as a relic at Christ Church Cathedral in Dublin before being burned to ashes in a nearby alleyway in 1538 (an event that precipitated riots), Artaud headed first by train for Galway rather than Dublin – the extensive Irish railway network of that era allowed for a direct journey from Cobh to Galway – and then by ferry to Inishmore. It's not known why he chose to travel especially to Inishmore, other than that he later told his editor of the 1940s, Paule Thévenin, that he had been deeply struck by Robert Flaherty's 1934 film *Man of Aran*, which was shot on Inishmore, and had been widely seen in cinemas in Paris. Up to the mid-1930s, and his travels to Mexico, Artaud remained deeply preoccupied with film; he made his living through film-acting, and frequently attempted to find the funding to direct films himself. With Inishmore's filmic human figures desperately attempting to survive on a desolate, sloping terrain of vast, cracked limestone slabs surrounded by wild seascapes of roaring waves, and with its outbursts of spectacular prehistoric drum-shaped clifftop hill-forts (to whose summits witnesses remembered Artaud climbing in order to look out westwards), the island as depicted in *Man of Aran* must have appeared an ideal location on which to envision and witness signs of his imminent Apocalypse. But many preoccupations and compulsions certainly formed an amalgam to make Artaud so determined to reach Inishmore.

Before leaving Paris, Artaud had written to Art Ó Briain, the Minister of the Irish Free State Legation there (in his letter, Artaud mentioned his interest in John Millington Synge, the Irish dramatist and author of *The Aran Islands*, 1907), and received in return a brief, non-committal letter of introduction which Artaud then used in Ireland as a form of currency, since he appears to have travelled with no money whatsoever, and to have undertaken his entire journey without ever paying for anything (though he was always interested in knowing how much things cost, and was preoccupied by the implausible possibility that he could persuade one or other of his friends in Paris to send him some money). For a lengthy period following Artaud's journey to Ireland, insistent but futile attempts were made to coerce the Minister who had issued that ill-advised letter of introduction, as well as Artaud's family, to agree to settle his debts, especially those for his accommodation on Inishmore (parts of the blackly comical bureaucratic correspondence relating to those claims for repayment are reproduced in an issue of the *Dublin Review*, issue 1, Winter 2000-01); no repayment of Artaud's costs was ever made.

Artaud stayed in the isolated hamlet of Eoghanacht, almost at the far end of the island from its port, Kilronan, in a room in the two-storey house of a lighthouse keeper, Sean Ó Milleáin, who lived there with his family. Artaud spoke very little English and no Gaelic. When I visited Eoghanacht in 2001, the weatherbeaten house was still there, though abandoned and dilapidated, as with most other houses in the hamlet, whose inhabitants preferred to live in caravans directly alongside their former homes. The lighthouse keeper appears to have treated Artaud well, and to have loaned him sums of money and to have not insisted on the immediate payment of his bill; one of his daughters, who had recently married and was around twenty years of age at the time, remembered fighting with Artaud in an interview with the researcher Peter Collier published in the *Irish Times* in 1997: 'There was something in the stick [Artaud's 'cane of St Patrick']. I was always play-acting to get it off him. My mother would shout after him: Stop chasing with that one as she's only married... But I was not afraid of him. The only thing was to keep away from the stick, but I suppose I was a devil, like himself.' Some children in the hamlet (now-aged figures, sixty-four years later, as they remembered Artaud's distinctive presence on Inishmore) threw stones at Artaud's feet as he walked at speed either to or from the island's hill-forts, while other children fearfully kept their distance from the forbidding figure they called 'the little Frenchman'. From the elevation of the nearest hill-fort to Artaud's lodgings, Dun Eoghanacht, it is possible to look both westwards out across the Atlantic Ocean, and also northwards along the coast of mainland Ireland. Other than taking walks to the hill-forts, Artaud wrote several letters, though most of his letters from Ireland actually date from later in his journey, and were sent from Galway and Dublin. He frequently walked the considerable distance to the post-office in Kilronan to see if anyone had sent him any money.

From Kilronan, Artaud eventually returned after around ten days (the precise date of his departure from Inishmore isn't known) on the ferry to Galway and stayed at the city's salubrious Imperial Hotel, amassing more unpaid debts and writing more letters, along with the first of the intentionally damaged and part-burnt magic spells – able to hold either maleficent or defensive powers, as curses or protections – which he continued to create over the following years spent in insane asylums, before leaving by train for Dublin on 8 September. There, his journey abruptly unravelled, to the extent that it had ever been under any degree of control. But he continued to write letters, even in those extreme conditions. He became destitute and stayed in hostels for the homeless, starving. He appears to have had several violent altercations with the Dublin police and to have been badly beaten in an incident on 18 September. He either lost his 'cane of St Patrick', or it was confiscated from him by the police and thrown away. He was arrested in Milltown Park (the large, wooded grounds of a Jesuit community's house to the south of Dublin's centre), interrogated in Mountjoy Prison, and deported from Ireland as an undesirable alien. Two policemen were assigned to accompany him on the train back to the port of Cobh and to put him on the ferry. Artaud's letters from Ireland end with his vision of the ugly-voiced Antichrist at the Deux Magots café back in Paris, and with Artaud's urgent need to create and send a magic spell to protect his friend, the young artist and dancer Sonia Mossé (who would herself be deported, from France, with the active complicity of the French police, and was murdered in 1943 at the Sobibor concentration camp); Artaud's corporeal journey to Ireland ended, eight days after his last letter, on 29 September, with his forcible expulsion.

On the overnight ferry back from Cobh to the French port of Le Havre, new violent altercations flared up since Artaud believed he was being threatened by attacks from the ferry's stewards. After being detained on his arrival in Le Havre on 30 September, he was taken to a lunatic asylum near the city of Rouen, and from there, on to numerous other asylums in different parts of France, over a period of nine years which encompassed the entirety of the Second World War and the Occupation of France by German forces, during which he was often in danger of starving to death, while suffering many beatings by asylum wardens, as well as undergoing fifty-one electroshock sessions administered by doctors at his final asylum, Rodez. Through the intervention of his friends, Artaud was finally released from the Rodez asylum, in rural south-central France, in 1946. Whenever he evoked his travels in Ireland to the director of the Rodez asylum, a young psychiatrist who had once been a Surrealist poet, Gaston Ferdière, Artaud spoke of a journey of terrifying brutality and solitude.

Along with Artaud's preoccupations in Ireland with his envisioned imminent Apocalypse and his seething animosity towards the writer and patron of the Surrealists, Lise Deharme – who had wounded him with barbed ridicule shortly before his departure for Ireland – Artaud was evidently deeply engaged with each of his six correspondents, and that engagement endured – in different and often negative ways – across the nine years of his subsequent asylum incarceration, when several of the correspondents of his Ireland letters visited him at one or other of his many asylums, notably at the Sainte-Anne and Ville-Evrard asylums which were located either in or on the edge of Paris. Artaud believed that Anie Besnard had been murdered by his adversaries and replaced by a double, and that it was the spectral double or 'demon' who now visited him at Ville-Evrard. Georgette Dunais (who appears in his letters under her journalistic pseudonym, Anne Manson), was abruptly dismissed by Artaud when she attempted to visit him in 1938 at Sainte-Anne, and she then reproached him in an unpublished letter that evokes their relationship in Paris immediately before Artaud's journey to Ireland: 'Artaud, I will come and see you on Sunday and you are not going to push me away because it's going to be too painful for me./This morning I was re-reading the letters which you wrote to me at the time when your friendship made all other friendships impossible./ Do you remember that you said to me: "I need something human, still?" – Well, I live in the human and I have need of your grandeur.' During his incarceration, Artaud appears to have forgotten about his hatred of Lise Deharme, as though by sending her a cigarette-burnt magic spell from the Imperial Hotel, Galway, he had expunged her from his life. At Rodez in 1943, Artaud told the asylum's director that he now saw his Apocalyptic prophecies of 1937 as being realised in the Second World War's immense conflagrations and massacres, but in a strangely faded-out and reduced way, like an irradiated film image, that could not compete with the virulence and all-engulfing scale of his own visions.

After his release from Rodez, Artaud lived for nearly two years in a ramshackle pavilion in the park of a convalescence-clinic in the south-eastern suburbs of Paris, at Ivry-sur-Seine, writing and drawing incessantly, and recording radio-programmes commissioned for the French national radio-station (the last of which was censored for obscenity and profanity, and was not transmitted). When he spoke of his journey to Ireland, during that final period, to new friends such as his young editor Paule Thévenin, Artaud's memories were again of a brutal, infernal experience. He died in 1948, at the age of fifty-one, in the early-morning hours of 4 March, after a night of falling snow, during which he had written his final text in one of the schoolchildren's exercise-books whose rough pages he habitually used for his texts in that final period: 'the same individual/ returns, then, each/morning (it's another)/to accomplish his/revolting, criminal/and murderous, sinister/task which is to/maintain/a state of *bewitchment* in/me/and to continue to/render me/an eternally/ bewitched man/etc etc'. He was found sitting upright on the edge of his bed, his shoe in his hand.

By examining the original, now semi-disintegrated artefacts of Artaud's letters from Ireland, in the archives and collections in which they are preserved, it's clear that he wrote them with great rapidity, though he sometimes used scraps of paper to work out particular phrases or passages in advance before inserting them into the letters. It's not known how many of Artaud's letters from Ireland are lost, but it must be a considerable number; several of his correspondents, such as Georgette Dunais, did not view the letters as objects that necessarily had to be carefully preserved, whereas André Breton systematically filed away Artaud's letters with the rest of his vast correspondence. Over thirty years passed between the sending of the letters to their correspondents (several of whom died in the interval), and their subsequent assembling for publication by Artaud's editor, Paule Thévenin. The two surviving magic spells from Artaud's journey to Ireland were undertaken with meticulous attention, and when he went on to create further spells at the asylums in which he was incarcerated over the following years, he used coloured crayons and pencils, and burned the spells' surfaces with his cigarettes in specific places; in recent decades, the spells have been exhibited, alongside Artaud's drawings of 1945–48, in the galleries of national art museums.

*

These translations of Artaud's letters from his Apocalyptic journey to Ireland are dedicated to the memory of Cathrin Pichler, who – together with Hans Peter Litscher – curated an extraordinary exhibition of Artaud's drawings, notebooks, letters and magic spells at the Vienna Museum of Modern Art in 2002. The translations are dedicated also to Paule Thévenin, Artaud's editor (and later the editor of Jean Genet, and a friend and supporter of Pierre Guyotat and Jacques Derrida), who was relentlessly impeded in her life's work of publishing Artaud's texts by his family 'heirs', and who would perhaps be satisfied that Artaud's work, seventy years after his death, is now entering the public domain. Curse all those who ever tried to silence Artaud.

Artaud in a street in Ivry-sur-Seine, January 1948
Photograph courtesy of Paule Thévenin

© DIAPHANES 2019
ISBN 978-3-0358-0153-8

ALL RIGHTS RESERVED

DIAPHANES
HARDSTR. 69 | CH-8004 ZURICH
DRESDENER STR. 118 | D-10999 BERLIN

PRINTED IN GERMANY
LAYOUT: 2EDIT, ZURICH

WWW.DIAPHANES.COM